United States Government Accountability Office

Report to Congressional Requesters

I0415766

February 2012

REPORTING FOREIGN ACCOUNTS TO IRS

Extent of Duplication Not Currently Known, but Requirements Can Be Clarified

GAO-12-403

Contents

Letter		1
Appendix I	Briefing Slides	5
Appendix II	GAO Contact and Staff Acknowledgments	32

Abbreviations

BSA	Bank Secrecy Act
FATCA	Foreign Account Tax Compliance Act
FBAR	Foreign Bank Account Report
FinCen	Financial Crimes Enforcement Network
IRC	Internal Revenue Code
IRS	Internal Revenue Service

G A O
Accountability * Integrity * Reliability

United States Government Accountability Office
Washington, DC 20548

February 28, 2012

The Honorable Max Baucus
Chairman
Committee on Finance
United States Senate

The Honorable Charles E. Grassley
Ranking Member
Committee on the Judiciary
United States Senate

This letter formally transmits the briefing we gave on February 1, 2012. We gave this briefing in response to your request that we assess potential duplicative foreign-account reporting requirements under the Foreign Account Tax Compliance Act (FATCA)[1] for the Internal Revenue Service (IRS) Form 8938 and under the Bank Secrecy Act (BSA) for the Foreign Bank Account Report (FBAR).[2]

The objectives of the briefing were to (1) determine to what extent, if any, the reporting requirements on the FATCA Form 8938 and FBAR are duplicative; (2) assess the potential effects that any duplicative reporting requirements have on filers; and (3) identify and assess opportunities, if any, to cost-effectively reduce or eliminate the burden that any duplicative reporting creates while maintaining the usefulness of the information for tax-administration and law-enforcement purposes.

To address objective 1, we analyzed and compared the statutes, regulations, forms, and guidance governing FATCA and FBAR reporting requirements. We identified areas in which filers are required to report the same or similar information. For objective 2, we spoke with and examined documentation from Treasury's Office of Tax Policy, IRS, the Financial Crimes Enforcement Network (FinCEN), and taxpayers and their

---

[1]FATCA was enacted in 2010 as part of the Hiring Incentives to Restore Employment Act, Pub. L. No. 111-147, 124 Stat. 71, title V, subtitle A (Mar. 18, 2010).

[2]Pub. L. No. 91-508, titles I and II, 84 Stat. 1114 (Oct. 26, 1970) (codified as amended at 12 U.S.C. § § 1829b, 1951-1959; 31 U.S.C. § § 5311-5322.

representatives to identify the amount of duplicative reporting they expect will result from the two reporting requirements. This included the perspectives of a range of taxpayers, tax practitioners with experience in reporting on the foreign financial activities of their clients, and organizations representing the interests of U.S. taxpayers that live in foreign countries.

Sufficient data were not available to estimate the number of filers that would have duplicative reporting requirements. For objective 3, we used our analysis of areas of duplication for objective 1 to determine whether changes could be made that would meet the following criteria:

- filer burden from duplicative reporting would be reduced or eliminated;
- usefulness of the information would be maintained for tax-administration and law-enforcement purposes—changes could not affect the substance of the reporting requirements including the deadlines for when forms must be filed; and
- implementation of the changes must be cost-effective—that is, costs must be less than the benefits that burden reduction or elimination would create.

We conducted this performance audit from September 2011 to February 2012 in accordance with generally accepted government auditing standards. Those standards require that we plan and perform the audit to obtain sufficient, appropriate evidence to provide a reasonable basis for our findings and conclusions based on our audit objectives. We believe that the evidence obtained provides a reasonable basis for our findings and conclusions based on our audit objectives.

In summary, some of the information requested on the Form 8938 and FBAR is duplicative, but the number of filers affected is not currently known. Since the Form 8938 and FBAR were developed to meet two different governmental needs—tax administration and law enforcement—some filers have to report the same or similar information twice, but through different mechanisms and at different times. This increases the compliance burden and adds complexity that can create confusion, potentially resulting in inaccurate or unnecessary reporting. Currently, the instructions and guidance for both forms lack any explanation of why and where duplication exists. Actions to reduce duplicate reporting requirements while maintaining the usefulness of the data for tax administration and law enforcement purposes would benefit filers. However, since the Form 8938 is a new requirement beginning after 2011, data are not yet available to determine the number of filers subject to these duplicative reporting requirements. Without these data, it is not known whether the benefits of reduced duplication would exceed the costs. When filing data become available, Treasury's Office of Tax Policy, IRS, and FinCEN would have the information needed to assess whether cost-effective steps could be taken, including allowing filers who would normally have to submit both forms to substitute the information reported on one to meet the requirements of the other. Hence, we are recommending that the Secretary of the Treasury direct the Office of Tax Policy, IRS, and FinCEN to (1) revise both the Form 8938 and FBAR instructions and related guidance to explain the extent to which duplication exists (for example, instances where account-related information requested on the two forms is the same or different) and the circumstances in which filers are, or are not, expected to comply with both reporting requirements; and (2) as data become available, determine whether the benefits of implementing a less-duplicative reporting process exceed the costs and if so, implement that process.

We provided a draft of this report to Treasury's Office of Tax Policy, IRS and FinCEN for official comment on February 2, 2012. IRS provided a number of technical comments that we have incorporated where appropriate. In addition, during our work we met with officials at all three agencies, all of whom provided technical feedback. None of the agencies provided written comments on the draft report or recommendations.

As agreed with your office, unless you publicly announce the contents of this report earlier, we plan no further distribution of this report until 30 days from the report date. At that time, we will send copies of this report to the appropriate congressional committees, the Commissioner of Internal Revenue, the Director of FinCEN, the Secretary of the Treasury, the Chairman of the IRS Oversight Board, and the Director of the Office of Management and Budget. Copies also are available at no charge on the GAO website at http://www.gao.gov.

If you or your staffs have any questions about this report, please contact me at (202) 512-9110 or whitej@gao.gov. Contact points for our offices of Congressional Relations and Public Affairs are on the last page of this report. GAO staff members who made major contributions to this report are listed in appendix II.

James R. White
Director, Tax Issues
Strategic Issues

Appendix I: Briefing Slides

REPORTING FOREIGN ACCOUNTS TO IRS: Extent of Duplication Not Currently Known, but Requirements Can Be Clarified

Briefing for Staffs of the Senate Committee on Finance (Majority) and Senator Grassley
February 1, 2012

Based on technical comments provided by IRS, minor updates were made to these materials after the briefing date.

For more information, contact James R. White at (202) 512-9110 or whitej@gao.gov   Page 1

Foreign Financial Accounts are Now Subject to Two Reporting Regimes for Two Purposes

- Congress, the Department of the Treasury (Treasury), the Internal Revenue Service (IRS), and others have expressed concerns over efforts by U.S. taxpayers to hide or disguise financial activities offshore. IRS does not have an estimate of the revenue loss due to offshore non-compliance, and estimates by others are unreliable. However, some international tax policy experts believe that the losses are in the billions of dollars annually.

- These tax administration concerns contributed to the passage of the Foreign Account Tax Compliance Act (FATCA), enacted in 2010 as part of the Hiring Incentives to Restore Employment Act.[1]
    - This legislation, which has several provisions, is an important development in efforts to combat tax evasion by U.S. persons holding investments in offshore accounts.
    - One provision requires U.S. persons holding foreign financial accounts and other foreign assets, such as stock investments in a foreign company, to report these items and the related income to IRS with their tax return on the Form 8938. [2]
    - It is expected that IRS will use this information to increase tax compliance.

[1]Pub. L. No. 111-147, 124 Stat. 71, title V, subtitle A (Mar. 18, 2010).
[2]26 U.S.C. § 6038D.

Page 2

Foreign Financial Accounts are Now Subject to Two Reporting Regimes (continued)

- The Bank Secrecy Act of 1970 (BSA) can be used by federal, state, and local law enforcement agencies to combat financial crimes, including terrorist financing and tax evasion.[3]
    - Under BSA, aspects of the self-reporting requirement under FATCA already exist.
    - Certain taxpayers and residents are required to file a TD F 90-22.1(commonly known as the Foreign Bank Accounts Report or FBAR) on financial accounts.
    - Unlike FATCA, information on other foreign financial assets are not reported.
    - FBAR information is managed by the Financial Crimes Enforcement Network (FinCEN).

- You asked us to examine the potential duplication in foreign financial account reporting and any burden this creates for filers.[4]

[3]Bank Secrecy Act, titles I and II of Pub. L No 91-508, 84 Stat. 1114 (1970), as amended, codified as 12 U.S.C. § § 1829b, 1951-1959, and 31 U.S.C. § § 5311-5322.

[4]This review only examines the self-reporting requirements under FATCA and, therefore, does not include the third party reporting requirements that are expected to apply to foreign financial institutions after 2012.

Page 3

Objectives

1. Determine to what extent, if any, the reporting requirements on the FATCA Form 8938 and FBAR are duplicative;

2. Assess the potential effects that any duplicative reporting requirements have on filers; and

3. Identify and assess opportunities, if any, to cost effectively reduce or eliminate the burden that any duplicative reporting creates while maintaining the usefulness of the information for tax administration and law-enforcement purposes.

Page 4

Results in Brief

- Some of the information requested on the Form 8938 and FBAR is duplicative. Both forms ask for the same or similar information on the filer, foreign financial accounts, and financial institutions where accounts are held. Form 8938 asks for additional information not required by the FBAR, such as other foreign financial assets and income. Since the Form 8938 is a new requirement beginning after 2011, data are not yet available to determine the number of filers subject to these duplicative reporting requirements.

- A variety of tax commentators, taxpayer representatives, and individuals stated that these duplicative reporting requirements have created confusion. They report being unclear about what and how information should be reported on both forms. Neither form provides filers any explanation as to why duplicative reporting is necessary, where the duplication occurs, or how the information being requested is the same or different.

- Without data on Form 8938 filers, the benefits and costs of taking actions to reduce duplicative reporting cannot be determined. When Form 8938 filing data becomes available, Treasury's Office of Tax Policy, IRS, and FinCEN would have the information needed to assess whether cost-effective steps could be taken, including allowing filers who would normally have to submit both forms to substitute the information reported on one to meet the requirements of the other.

Page 5

GAO-12-403 Reporting Foreign Accounts to IRS

Scope and Methodology

- For objective 1, we analyzed and compared the statutes, regulations, forms and guidance governing FATCA and FBAR filing requirements. We did not review the FATCA requirements that apply to 3rd party reporting by foreign financial institutions.

- For objective 2, we spoke with and examined documentation from Treasury's Office of Tax Policy, IRS, FinCEN, and taxpayers and their representatives to identify the amount of duplicative reporting they expect will result from the two reporting requirements. Sufficient data are not available to estimate the number of filers that would have duplicative reporting requirements.

- For objective 3, we used our analysis of areas of duplication for objective 1 to determine whether changes could be made that would meet the following criteria:
    - filer burden from duplicative reporting would be reduced or eliminated;
    - usefulness of the information must be maintained for tax administration and law-enforcement purposes—changes could not affect the substance of the reporting requirements including the deadlines for when forms must be filed; and
    - implementation of the changes must be cost effective—i.e., costs must be less than the benefits that burden reduction or elimination would create.

Page 6

Background

- Beginning in 2012, certain taxpayers with foreign financial accounts and other foreign financial assets above applicable thresholds must report this information with their income tax return on Form 8938.
  - Thresholds triggering the reporting requirement vary depending on the filer type and whether they reside domestically or abroad.
  - Other exceptions also exist that would limit the filing requirement, such as accounts held in financial institutions that are considered U.S. payers (e.g., a foreign branch of a U.S.-based financial institution).
  - Like most income tax filings, the Form 8938 is included with a timely filed tax return, which is generally filed by April 15, but in certain cases can be extended to as late as December 15 for some taxpayers that reside outside the United States.
  - Filers who do not comply with this requirement could be subject to monetary penalties, as described in supplement 1 of this briefing.
  - Like all tax information, IRS is generally prohibited from disclosing information provided on Form 8938 under section 6103 of the Internal Revenue Code (IRC) unless an exception applies.

Page 7

Background

- Under BSA, U.S. residents or citizens are required to keep records and file reports on transactions with foreign financial institutions. Administration of this requirement was delegated to FinCEN, which established regulations requiring those with a financial interest or signature authority over one or more foreign financial accounts with a total of more than $10,000 to annually file an FBAR with Treasury.[5]
  - The FBAR must be filed for the calendar year by June 30th of the following year, with no extension allowed.
  - Unlike the Form 8938, other foreign assets such as stock investments in foreign companies and income are not required to be reported on the FBAR.
  - The FBAR, however, does require certain accounts to be reported that are not required on Form 8938, such as accounts that the filer does not own but has been designated control over the funds in the account through signature authority.
  - BSA information is used by law enforcement to combat financial crimes, such as tax evasion, money laundering, and terrorist financing.
  - Information reported under BSA is not tax information and, therefore, not protected from disclosure under IRC § 6103.
  - Noncompliance with FBAR can result in penalties, as shown in supplement 1.

- Figure 1 illustrates how information is reported and used under FATCA and FBAR.

[5]31 C.F.R. § 1010.350.

Page 8

Background
Figure 1: Illustration of Information Reporting under FATCA and FBAR

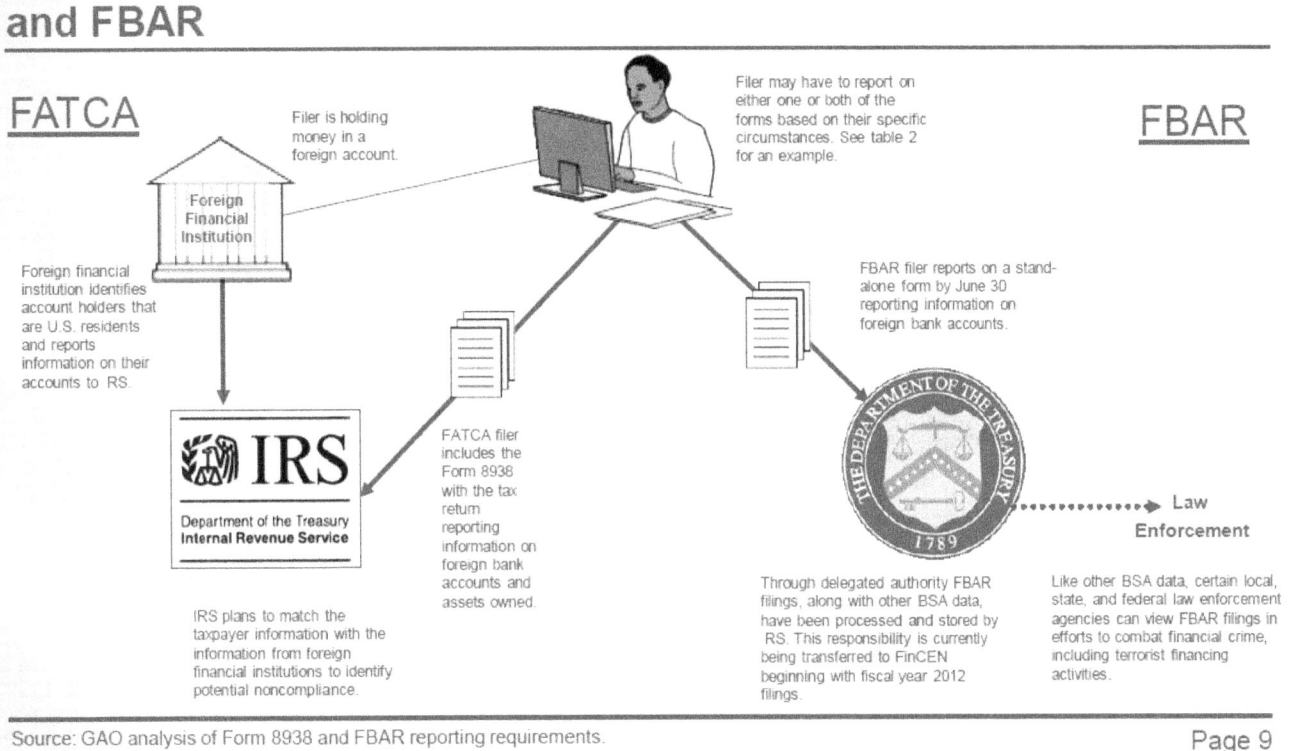

Source: GAO analysis of Form 8938 and FBAR reporting requirements.

Page 9

Background

- While the authority to administer BSA was delegated to FinCEN by Treasury, IRS plays an important role in FBAR administration. FinCEN delegated to IRS its authority to enforce the FBAR requirements in April of 2003. As a result, IRS currently interprets FBAR law when issuing administrative rulings, examining FBAR cases, and assessing FBAR penalties.

- According to IRS officials, they do not regularly coordinate with FinCEN when examining cases or assessing penalties.

- Although FBAR enforcement authority was delegated, FinCEN maintains its authority to issue FBAR regulations. However, IRS has responsibility for revising the FBAR form and instructions.

Page 10

Form 8938 and FBAR Reporting Requirements Are Duplicative for Some Filers

- As shown by comparing the forms in figure 2 and the instructions in table 1, part 1 of the Form 8938 duplicates most of the information requested on the FBAR.
  - The form language and instructions for both forms use terminology that is exactly the same, or duplicative, for information on the identity of the filer, the account type and value, and the financial institution where the account is held.
  - The forms and instructions also use terminology that is not exactly the same, but is similar—the forms and instructions have similar definitions. For example, the Form 8938 asks whether the filer is a married individual filing jointly or as an "other" individual. The FBAR asks whether the filer is reporting as an individual.

- Parts 2, 3, and 4 of the Form 8938 ask for information not required on the FBAR—
  - Part 2 requests information on other foreign financial assets.
  - Part 3 requests information on income generated by the items.
  - Part 4 asks for information on the other tax forms where foreign financial assets are reported that are not included on the Form 8938.

Page 11

Figure 2: Duplicative or Similar Reporting Requirements

Source: GAO analysis of the Form 8938 and FBAR

Page 12

Note: The entire Form 8938 can be found here: http://www.irs.gov/pub/irs-pdf/f8938.pdf and the FBAR here: http://www.fincen.gov/forms/files/f9022-1_fbar.pdf.

Table 1: Areas of Duplication in Form 8938 and FBAR Instructions

	Form 8938	FBAR	Duplication
Type of filer	Individual (U.S. citizens, resident aliens and some nonresident aliens) or any domestic entity holding, directly or indirectly, specified foreign financial assets. (Domestic entities are not subject to this filing until final regulations are issued)	U.S. person (U.S. citizens; U.S. residents; entities, including but not limited to, corporations, partnerships, or limited liability companies created or organized in the United States or under laws of the United States; and trusts or estates formed under the laws of the United States).	An individual, U.S. citizen, or resident, in many cases will also be a U.S. person.
Time period covered	Taxable year.	Calendar year.	Taxable and calendar year, in the case of most individual filers, are the same.
Type of interest in foreign financial accounts/ assets	Specified interest in a foreign financial asset.	Financial interest in, or signature authority over, foreign financial accounts.	In many cases specified interest as defined in the Form 8938 instructions will be the same as the financial interest under FBAR.
Currency conversion	Document the foreign currency exchange rate used and document the source of that rate if it is not the U.S. Treasury Financial Management Service.	Use the Treasury's Financial Management Service's conversion rate, unless it is not available. If it is not available, use another verifiable rate and provide the source of that rate.	Both forms require currency to be converted to U.S. dollars and documentation of the source of that rate if it is not the U.S. Treasury Financial Management Service.

Source: GAO analysis of the Form 8938 and FBAR instructions.

Page 13

Table 1: Areas of Duplication in Form 8938 and FBAR Instructions (continued)

	Form 8938	FBAR	Duplication
Value making foreign account/ asset reportable	Aggregate value of all assets exceeds:[a] -$50,000 - $200,000 for US residents - $200,000 - $600,000 for foreign residents.	Aggregate value of reportable accounts (including both financial interest and signature authority) exceeds $10,000.	Assets on the Form 8938 includes financial accounts. Therefore, in many cases financial accounts that, in aggregate, exceed $10,000 have to be reported on both forms if the minimum Form 8938 thresholds are exceeded.
Type of foreign financial accounts/ assets reportable	1. Any financial account maintained by a foreign financial institution. 2. Any of the following assets which are not held in an account maintained by a financial institution— A. Any stock or security issued by a person other than a U.S. person. B. Any financial instrument or contract held for investment that has an issuer or counterparty which is other than a U.S. person. C. Any interest in a foreign entity.	Bank account, securities account, or other financial account in a foreign country. Term also includes savings, demand, checking, deposit, time deposit, or other account maintained with a financial institution or other person engaged in the business of a financial institution.	Bank, securities, and other financial accounts as defined under FBAR, in many cases, would include financial accounts maintained by a foreign financial institution as defined for the Form 8938.

Source: GAO analysis of the Form 8938 and FBAR instructions.

[a] Different thresholds apply based on whether a filer files a joint income tax return or resides outside the United States., and whether asset values exceed a certain threshold at any point during the year. If the end of year aggregate value filing threshold is not met, a higher threshold applies during the year .

Page 14

Exceptions to Form 8938 Reporting Requirements Reduce Duplicative Reporting

- Treasury's Office of Tax Policy and IRS have worked to reduce the number of taxpayers that have to file the Form 8938 by creating several exceptions that do not exist in the FBAR requirements. These exceptions include:
  - Filers that do not have a tax filing obligation;
  - Filers that have already reported the foreign account information on another specified tax form;
  - Accounts held in a foreign financial institution deemed a U.S. payer (e.g., a foreign branch or foreign subsidiary of a U.S. financial institution); and
  - Accounts held by a resident in a U.S. possession, where the financial institution is also in that U.S. possession (American Samoa, Guam, the Northern Mariana Islands, Puerto Rico, or the U.S. Virgin Islands).

Page 15

Table 2: Dollar Values Are Another Factor in Determining Duplicate Reporting (assuming no exceptions)

Filer Situation (Individual U.S. Resident)[a]	Filing Requirements[b]
Foreign account values are greater than $50,000 and:	
No other foreign financial assets	**Form 8938 part 1 and FBAR**
Other foreign financial assets	**Form 8938 part 1 and 2 and FBAR**
Foreign account value are between $10,000 and $50,000 and:	
No other foreign financial assets	FBAR
Account and other foreign financial asset values are below $50,000	FBAR
Account and other foreign financial asset values are above $50,000	**Form 8938 part 1 and 2 and FBAR**
Foreign account values are below $10,000 and:	
No other foreign financial assets	No reporting
Account and other foreign financial asset values are below $10,000	No reporting
Foreign account and other foreign financial asset values are between $10,000 and $50,000	No reporting
Account and other foreign financial asset values are above $50,000	Form 8938 part 1 and 2
Foreign account values are zero and:	
Other foreign financial asset values are below $50,000	No reporting
Other foreign financial asset values are above $50,000	Form 8938 part 2

[a]Filers in other situations, such as individuals that are married filing jointly or who reside in a foreign country, would be subject to different filing thresholds on the Form 8938.

[b]In most cases where filers have to fill out the Form 8938 parts 1 or 2, they will also have to report income in part 3. In some cases filers will not fill out part 2 if they have already reported to IRS elsewhere. Instead, they would indicate this in part 4.

Source: GAO analysis of Form 8938 and FBAR requirements.

Note: **Bold text** indicates situations in which the filer would have duplicative reporting requirements.

Page 16

IRS is Uncertain About How Many Filers Will Be Subject to Duplicative Filing Requirements

- Since the Form 8938 is a new requirement beginning in the 2012 filing year, IRS does not have data on how many Form 8938 filers will also need to file an FBAR.

- Past FBAR filings cannot be used to produce a valid estimate of the number of filers subject to duplicate reporting requirements because several pieces of data are not available, such as—
    - Data on the other foreign financial assets of FBAR filers. As shown in table 2, there are FBAR filers with financial accounts that fall short of the Form 8938 reporting threshold but who may also have other foreign financial assets that would result in the filer exceeding that threshold; and
    - Data on some of the exceptions to the Form 8938 reporting requirement. For example, data is not available on how many FBAR filers reported foreign financial account information in another part of the tax return instead of the Form 8938.

Page 17

Some Filers and Their Representatives Expressed Concerns Over the Impact of Duplicative Reporting Requirements

- We talked to several tax professionals and reviewed articles in the tax press. In addition, we reviewed comments received by IRS on a proposed draft of the Form 8938.[6] The sources of those comments included three representatives of organizations whose members are overseas taxpayers, four tax practitioners representing their clients, 12 individual taxpayers, and 8 who were unknown. Although not representative of the population of filers, we identified several common concerns over duplication, including:
    - additional time and cost burden to obtain and maintain records and file both forms,
    - confusion over similarities and differences in terminology and the implications for what and how information should be reported,
    - concern over exposure to two different penalty regimes for essentially the same information (details on the penalty regimes are in supplement 1), and
    - different filing deadlines (i.e. June 30th for FBAR and between April 15th and December 15th, depending on extensions, for FATCA).

- Some commentators noted the obvious overlap in requirements, as evidenced by their use of terms like the "Tax FBAR" or "Super FBAR" when referring to the Form 8938.

[6]Comments were received prior to the issuance of the IRC Section 6038D regulations and the final version of Form 8938 and the accompanying instructions.

Page 18

Some Filers and Their Representatives Expressed Concerns Over the Impact of Overlapping Reporting Requirements (continued)

- Selected quotes from written comments on the draft Form 8938:

- "...if the FBAR is not sufficient for the IRS and the Department of Treasury (sic), and this form is used as a replacement, that is fine, but don't keep both, this is not right and not fair."

- "(Part 1) is all information submitted to (T)reasury on (the FBAR), does this mean we won't have to file this form anymore? As doing it twice is not an appetizing thought...."

- "...I wonder if the information in (Part 1) is not redundant to what we already have to report. It may not be all that good an idea to require essentially duplicative reporting."

- "...and it is in addition to (the FBAR), so not only is there a duplication of effort, but it is not clear how much overlap there is or if the forms are looking for different things."

- "The information is being reported to the Secretary of the Treasury on two different forms, then one or the other is unnecessary duplication of effort and one or the other should be abolished immediately."

Page 19

Duplicative Reporting Requirements Resulted From Two Parts of Treasury Developing Separate Forms, One for Tax Administration and the Other For Law-enforcement Purposes

- Treasury has duplicative foreign account reporting requirements because the laws that established them were passed at different times, under different parts of the U.S. Code, and to achieve different goals.
  - The Form 8938 requirement became law in 2010, whereas requirements for the FBAR were established in 1970.
  - The Form 8938 was established in the IRC which IRS administers, whereas FBAR requirements were established under BSA which FinCEN administers.
  - Use of the Form 8938 is generally limited to tax compliance, whereas FBAR information is used to combat financial crimes, which can include tax evasion, money laundering and terrorist financing.

- Reporting the same information on two different forms creates additional costs to the government to process the same or similar information twice and enforce reporting compliance with both requirements. The extent of these costs is not known. Enforcement costs would vary according to the level of effort employed by IRS.

Page 20

GAO
Accountability * Integrity * Reliability

Although the Burden of Duplicative Reporting is Not Yet Fully Known, Actions Could be Taken to Reduce Confusion

- Treasury's Office of Tax Policy and IRS have worked to reduce the number of taxpayers that have to file the Form 8938. However, actions have not been taken to reduce or eliminate the burden on filers that are subject to both requirements, in part, because data are not yet available to determine how many of these filers exist.

- Some actions could be taken before this data are available. Currently, neither the Form 8938 nor FBAR instructions or related guidance provides filers an explanation as to why duplicative reporting is necessary, where duplication occurs, or how the information being requested is the same or different.
    - As noted earlier, commentators pointed to these issues as a source of confusion.
    - Clarifying these issues in the instructions could reduce confusion and, therefore, compliance burden because filers could better understand the circumstances in which they are, or are not, expected to report the same information twice.
    - Clarifying these instructions would not impose costs on filers and would not require changes to the requirements or the forms.
    - Clarifying instructions, however, would not reduce the number of filers subject to duplicative reporting.

Page 21

Options Exist for Reducing Duplicative Reporting While Maintaining Usefulness, But Costs and Benefits are Not Known

- We were able to identify two options that have potential to reduce duplicative reporting. These options would allow filers who would normally have to submit both forms to substitute the information reported on one to meet the requirements of the other. Specifically:
    1. Allow eligible filers to substitute the FBAR for part 1 of Form 8938 as the information source on foreign financial accounts; and/or
    2. Allow eligible filers to substitute part 1 of Form 8938 as the information source on foreign financial accounts for the FBAR.

- Both options would allow eligible filers to choose to allow the information they report on one form or the other to meet both sets of reporting requirements without any changes to those requirements. Both options would:
    - reduce overall burden since eligible filers would only have to report foreign account information in one place; and
    - maintain the usefulness of the information for tax administration and law-enforcement purposes since the information reported would have to meet both sets of requirements, including filing deadlines.

Page 22

Both Options to Reduce Duplicative Reporting Have Implementation Costs, But They Are Unknown

- Either option would require changes in policies, processes, and systems to allow information reported on one form to be substituted for information on the other. Examples—
  - The system for sharing data between IRS and FinCEN would require modification.
  - Filers would need to be educated about any changes.

- To maintain the usefulness of the information reported for tax administration and law-enforcement purposes, options exist that could satisfy standing statutory and regulatory requirements but implementation details would have to be worked out and agreed to by IRS and FinCEN. These standing requirements, which differ for FBAR and FATCA, include:
  - filing due dates;
  - statutes of limitations;
  - penalties for missing filing requirements; and
  - taxpayer data and other privacy protections.

- Resolving these issues would have costs, many of them would be one time transition costs. IRS officials said these issues could be resolved, but were not sure of the costs.

Page 23

Whether Benefits of Either Option Would Outweigh Implementation Costs is Also Unknown

- Without estimated or actual data on the number of filers subject to duplicate filing requirements, the actual benefit that filers would receive from eliminating that requirement is unknown. This data would be needed to estimate the total costs in time and expense filers experience from having to comply with duplicative reporting requirements, and therefore, the benefits filers would receive from eliminating this duplication.

- Without agency-based analyses, there is no information on what the costs would be to implement new policies, procedures, processes, and systems for allowing information reported on one form to be substituted for and integrated with information reported on another.

Page 24

Conclusions

- The Form 8938 and FBAR were developed to meet two different governmental needs—tax administration and law enforcement. As a result, some filers have to report the same or similar information twice, but through different mechanisms and at different times.

- This increases compliance burden and adds complexity that can create confusion, potentially resulting in inaccurate or unnecessary reporting. Currently, the instructions and guidance for both forms lack any explanation of why and where duplication exists.

- Actions to reduce duplicate reporting requirements while maintaining their usefulness for tax administration and law-enforcement purposes would benefit filers. However, until Form 8938 filing data is available, it is not known whether these benefits would exceed the costs of implementation.

Page 25

Recommendation for Executive Action

- We recommend that the Secretary of the Treasury direct the Office of Tax Policy, IRS, and FinCEN to—

  1. Revise both the Form 8938 and FBAR instructions and related guidance to explain the extent to which duplication exists (for example, instances where financial account-related information requested on the two forms is the same or different) and the circumstances in which filers are, or are not, expected to comply with both reporting requirements, and

  2. As data becomes available, determine whether the benefits of implementing a less duplicative reporting process exceed the costs and if so, implement that process.

Page 26

Supplement 1
Table 3: Comparison of Form 8938 and FATCA Penalty
Regimes

	Form 8938	FBAR
Failure to File	$10,000	Maximum of $10,000
Continuing Failure to File	After 90 days from notice, an additional $10,000 for each 30 day period. Maximum additional penalty is $50,000	not applicable
Reasonable cause exception	Yes	Yes
Accuracy-related penalty	40 percent of the underpaid tax amount	not applicable.
Willful failure to file or willfully causing another to fail to file	not applicable	$100,000 or 50% of the account balance, whichever is greater
Fraud	75 percent of the underpaid tax amount attributable to fraud	not applicable
Criminal Penalties	Yes	Yes
Statute of Limitations	3 years after the date of filing or from when the information is reported to IRS and 6 years after the return was filed if the taxpayer fails to report over $5,000 in gross income from foreign assets	6 years to assess penalty and 2 additional years to collect after assessment

Source: GAO analysis of Form 8938 and FBAR instructions.

Page 27

Appendix II: GAO Contact and Staff Acknowledgments

GAO Contact	James R. White, (202) 512-9110, whitej@gao.gov
Staff Acknowledgments	In addition to the contact named above, Tom Short, Assistant Director; Amy Bowser; George Guttman; Brian James; John Mingus; and Cynthia Saunders made key contributions to this report.

GAO's Mission	The Government Accountability Office, the audit, evaluation, and investigative arm of Congress, exists to support Congress in meeting its constitutional responsibilities and to help improve the performance and accountability of the federal government for the American people. GAO examines the use of public funds; evaluates federal programs and policies; and provides analyses, recommendations, and other assistance to help Congress make informed oversight, policy, and funding decisions. GAO's commitment to good government is reflected in its core values of accountability, integrity, and reliability.
Obtaining Copies of GAO Reports and Testimony	The fastest and easiest way to obtain copies of GAO documents at no cost is through GAO's website (www.gao.gov). Each weekday afternoon, GAO posts on its website newly released reports, testimony, and correspondence. To have GAO e-mail you a list of newly posted products, go to www.gao.gov and select "E-mail Updates."
Order by Phone	The price of each GAO publication reflects GAO's actual cost of production and distribution and depends on the number of pages in the publication and whether the publication is printed in color or black and white. Pricing and ordering information is posted on GAO's website, http://www.gao.gov/ordering.htm. Place orders by calling (202) 512-6000, toll free (866) 801-7077, or TDD (202) 512-2537. Orders may be paid for using American Express, Discover Card, MasterCard, Visa, check, or money order. Call for additional information.
Connect with GAO	Connect with GAO on Facebook, Flickr, Twitter, and YouTube. Subscribe to our RSS Feeds or E-mail Updates. Listen to our Podcasts. Visit GAO on the web at www.gao.gov.
To Report Fraud, Waste, and Abuse in Federal Programs	Contact: Website: www.gao.gov/fraudnet/fraudnet.htm E-mail: fraudnet@gao.gov Automated answering system: (800) 424-5454 or (202) 512-7470
Congressional Relations	Katherine Siggerud, Managing Director, siggerudk@gao.gov, (202) 512-4400, U.S. Government Accountability Office, 441 G Street NW, Room 7125, Washington, DC 20548
Public Affairs	Chuck Young, Managing Director, youngc1@gao.gov, (202) 512-4800 U.S. Government Accountability Office, 441 G Street NW, Room 7149 Washington, DC 20548